WILTSHI

VACATION GUIDE
2023

The Essential and Ultimate Guide to St. Lucia's

Hotels, Cuisines, Shopping Tips, Insider's Tips,

Top Attractions, History and Culture

ALFRED FLORES

Copyright © 2023, Alfred Flores

TABLE OF CONTENTS

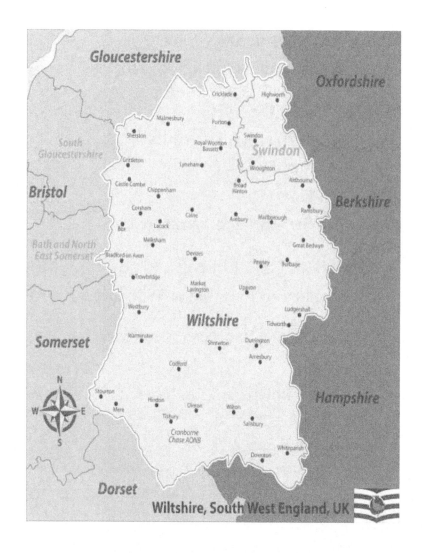

Vector map of Wiltshire in South West England, United Kingdom with regions and cities.

INTRODUCTION

Welcome to Wiltshire, an amazing county where history, untouched landscapes, and undiscovered gems join together to create a genuinely outstanding travel destination. Wiltshire is a compelling region of southwest England that is home to several historic sites, vast open spaces, and charming villages. This travel manual is your key to discovering the mysteries of Wiltshire, whether you are a die-hard history fan, a nature lover, or just looking for a quiet getaway.

You will go on a historical journey through the pages that come, learning about Wiltshire's colorful past and present as you go. The remnants of ancient civilizations can be found everywhere, from the famous Stonehenge stone circle to the mysterious Avebury stone circles. Discover a glimpse of Wiltshire's interesting past as you tour awe-inspiring castles, stunning cathedrals, and quaint market towns.

Wiltshire, however, is a place with spectacular natural beauty as well as a domain of the past. Large swaths of undulating hills, lush meadows, and historic woodlands beckon you to take in the natural splendor of the surroundings. Find more about the secluded valleys, serene lakes, and meandering rivers that thread through the countryside and provide chances for outdoor excursions and peaceful moments.

To help you get the most out of your trip to Wiltshire, we've carefully produced this thorough guidebook. We have compiled a variety of information to help you put up an unforgettable schedule, whether you're organizing a weekend break, a family holiday, or a lengthy exploration. We have gone above and beyond to provide you a really immersive and memorable experience. From in-depth descriptions of must-see attractions to off-the-beaten-path recommendations, from useful travel advice to insider recommendations, we have left no stone unturned.

You will find a wide variety of experiences in Wiltshire as you browse through the pages of this guide. Discover the hidden treasures nestled away in quaint towns, indulge in regional cuisine in quaint taverns and upscale restaurants, and make friends with the kind-hearted residents who proudly call this county home. Wiltshire offers a seductive vacation that will leave you craving more, whether you are enthralled by the mysteries of the past, revived by the splendor of nature, or just looking for a break from the chaos of modern life.

So come along with us as we explore Wiltshire's beauties on this amazing journey. This guide will be your dependable travel companion as you explore Wiltshire, revealing the beauty and charm that make the county a really unique travel destination, from its famous landmarks to its secret hideaways, historical riches to its natural splendors. The journey has begun!

CHAPTER ONE:
Getting to Know Wiltshire

Wiltshire is a charming county in the southwest of England that is renowned for its varied topography and illustrious past. Six counties, namely Gloucestershire, Oxfordshire, Berkshire, Hampshire, Dorset, and Somerset, round its 1,346 square miles (3,488 square kilometers) of land area. Major cities like London, Bristol, and Southampton can readily reach the county thanks to its center location within England.

Rolling hills, scenic valleys, and flowing rivers make up Wiltshire's topography. The Salisbury Plain, a sizable chalk plateau known for its historical significance and natural beauty, is located in the county. This well-known monument is home to various ancient ruins, including the famed Stonehenge and Avebury stone circles, in addition to being a haven for animals.

Along with its picturesque scenery, Wiltshire is home to a number of lovely market towns and villages, each with its own distinct personality. Salisbury, Marlborough, and Bradford-on-Avon are just a few places that have beautiful architecture, thriving marketplaces, and strong local cultures. These towns provide visitors a glimpse of traditional English living and act as entry points for discovering the nearby natural attractions.

Southern England's typical coastal climate is present in Wiltshire. The area experiences pleasant summers and cold winters, making it a desirable vacation spot all year round. Although the weather might change, Wiltshire generally has rather mild temperatures.

Wiltshire experiences summertime temperatures that often vary from 18°C to 22°C (64°F to 72°F) from June to August. Longer daylight hours during this season provide you plenty of time for outdoor activities and exploration. With blossoming wildflowers and rich green sceneries, the countryside is at its most colorful.

Wiltshire is painted in a tapestry of warm hues during the autumn (September to November) as the leaves change color. There is a progressive drop in temperature, with readings between 12°C and 17°C (54°F and 63°F). It's a lovely time to travel, especially if you're looking for peace and a chance to experience nature's amazing metamorphosis.

Temperatures drop during the winter (December to February), with typical highs between 7°C and 10°C (45°F and 50°F). Snowfall in Wiltshire is rather infrequent, but when it does, the countryside acquires a calm beauty, and the quaint charm of the towns and villages is even more enticing. Holiday markets and wintertime activities enhance the wintertime atmosphere.

Wiltshire comes to life in the spring (March to May) as flowers bloom and the countryside emerges from its winter slumber. Average temperatures range from 10°C to 15°C (50°F to 59°F), rising gradually. The weather is favorable for outdoor exploration during this time of year, and Wiltshire's gardens and parks offer a colorful backdrop.

As a result, it is advised to check the forecast closer to your trip because weather patterns might be unpredictable. Furthermore, Wiltshire's varied geography can produce microclimates, thus the weather may differ slightly depending on which part of the county you are in. No matter the time of year, Wiltshire's magnificence is evident, providing tourists with an enthralling and constantly-changing setting for their explorations.

Wiltshire is rich in history and has a tens of thousands of years' worth of cultural legacy. Ancient civilizations, medieval empires, and key historical events have all left their mark on the county's past. Wiltshire is a veritable gold mine for history buffs, with everything from ancient wonders to medieval masterpieces.

Stonehenge, a UNESCO World Heritage Site and one of the most recognizable prehistoric structures in the world, is one of Wiltshire's most well-known sites. This intriguing stone circle, which is said to have been built approximately 2500 BC, continues to enthrall tourists with its mystery origins and heavenly alignments. The fascinating Avebury stone circles, a collection of Neolithic and Bronze Age structures that includes the largest stone circle in Europe, are located close to Stonehenge.

The historic city of Salisbury, known for its majestic Salisbury Cathedral, is also located in the county. This architectural wonder from the 13th century houses the original Magna Carta and has the tallest spire in all of England. One can get a peek of Wiltshire's ancient history by strolling through Salisbury's cobblestone alleyways and stopping by its bustling market area.

The cultural heritage of Wiltshire goes beyond its historic sites. With several galleries, theaters, and cultural festivals devoted to the arts, the county is well renowned for its thriving arts sector. Local theaters present a wide range of acts, from plays and musicals to live music concerts, while artisans and artists demonstrate their skills.

Throughout the year, Wiltshire holds a number of festivals and events that highlight the county's rich cultural diversity, traditional customs, and thriving sense of community. These events provide guests a chance to experience Wiltshire's unique traditions firsthand and make lifelong memories.

The Salisbury International Arts Festival, which takes place every year in late spring, is one of the most well-known occasions in Wiltshire. This well-known event brings together artists from all over the world and offers a diverse lineup of performing, visual, and literary arts. The festival offers a vibrant and varied cultural experience by showcasing both established and up-and-coming artists.

Wiltshire comes alive in the summer with a variety of events honoring anything from literature and music to food and drink. The Larmer Tree Festival is a fascinating blend of music, comedy, theater, and family entertainment in the picturesque Larmer Tree Gardens. The Marlborough Food and Drink Festival, a display of regional produce, gourmet treats, and artisanal creations, is open to food and beverage enthusiasts.

Market towns in Wiltshire hold a number of other customary occasions all year long that pay homage to the region's agricultural heritage. There is always something to celebrate and enjoy, from classic country shows and agricultural festivals to Christmas markets and seasonal activities.

By participating in these celebrations, you may engage with the local population, consume delectable food, hear live music, and practice traditional practices while also getting a taste of Wiltshire's lively culture.

In conclusion, Wiltshire's varied landscape—from gentle hills to quaint market towns—along with its pleasant climate make it a desirable vacation spot all year round. Wiltshire provides a rich tapestry of experiences that will enthrall you, whether you choose to explore historic sites or immerse yourself in the peaceful countryside. The county's rich tapestry of history, culture, and events promises an educational and unique experience, whether you are enthralled by Wiltshire's ancient history, keen to explore its cultural legacy, or looking to rejoice with the people.

CHAPTER TWO: Planning Your Trip to Wiltshire

No of the time of year, Wiltshire is a popular travel destination due to its distinctive charm and beauty. Your own preferences and the experiences you're looking for will determine the ideal time to visit.

Due to the increased daylight hours and comfortable temperatures ranging from 18°C to 22°C (64°F to 72°F), the summer (June to August) is a popular season to visit Wiltshire. There are many outdoor activities available, and the environment is alive with vivid colors. It's a great time to go hiking, biking, and to visit historical monuments, gardens, and other places.

The weather is temperate, with temperatures ranging from 12°C to 17°C (54°F to 63°F), and the autumn (September to November) season covers Wiltshire in a tapestry of warm hues. This time of year is ideal for taking leisurely strolls through stunning scenery, taking in the peace and quiet of the countryside, and taking part in harvest celebrations and activities.

In Wiltshire, winter (December to February) gives a warm and wonderful atmosphere. The towns and villages come alive with holiday decorations, and you may immerse yourself in the splendor of Christmas markets and seasonal festivities as the temperature ranges from 7°C to 10°C (45°F to 50°F). A great season to see historical places and indoor attractions is the winter.

Wiltshire experiences a new lease on life from March to May as flowers bloom and the countryside awakens. Gradually rising temperatures range from 10°C to 15°C (50°F to 59°F). This time of year is great for strolling around beautiful gardens, taking in the colorful energy of springtime festivities, and enjoying breathtaking hikes.

Visa and Travel Requirements

It is crucial for visitors contemplating a trip to Wiltshire to check the necessary travel documents and visas for your country of residence. Citizens of several nations, including the United States, Canada, Australia, New

Zealand, and the majority of European countries, are exempt from visa requirements for short-term tourist visits to the United Kingdom, which includes Wiltshire, as of my knowledge cutoff in September 2021.

For the most recent information on visa requirements, it is advised to check the UK government's official website or contact your local embassy or consulate. Make sure your passport is valid for at least six months after the day you intend to depart.

It is important to keep in mind that immigration laws can change, therefore it is crucial to be updated and make plans as necessary to guarantee a simple and trouble-free trip to Wiltshire.

Wiltshire has good access to numerous means of transportation thanks to its convenient transportation connections.

- By Air: Bristol Airport (BRS) and London Heathrow Airport (LHR) are the closest international airports to Wiltshire. You can use a rail, bus, or vehicle to get to Wiltshire from these airports. Many minor airports, such Bournemouth Airport (BOH) and Southampton Airport (SOU), have domestic and international flights as well, giving passengers additional options.

- By Train: Direct connections from London and other significant cities provide excellent train service to Wiltshire. Salisbury, Swindon, Chippenham, and Trowbridge are among the major train hubs in Wiltshire. These stations offer quick access to many locations both within the county and elsewhere.

- By Car: With significant road networks linking Wiltshire to other regions of the UK, the county is simple to reach by automobile. The two main thoroughfares to Wiltshire are the M4 freeway and the A303 road. Before starting your travel, it is advisable to check for any active roadworks or traffic updates.

- By Bus: Bus services link Wiltshire with towns and counties close by. There are services to important towns and sites in

Wiltshire provided by National Express and local bus companies.

Once in Wiltshire, visitors can use buses and trains to travel about the county and get to their desired locations. But with a rental car, you have more freedom to stray from the usual path and take your time discovering the lovely countryside.

Getting Around

Wiltshire has a variety of ways to move around and discover its beautiful landscapes and quaint villages.

- Public transportation: Wiltshire has a robust public transportation system, which includes buses and trains and makes it easy to move about the county. Buses connect significant towns and villages, making it easy to go to well-known destinations and discover new areas. Train services offer quick links to the main train stations in Wiltshire, making it simple to get to places both inside and outside of the county.

- Car Rental: Renting a car in Wiltshire gives you the greatest degree of freedom and allows you to tour the area at your own speed. There are offices for car rental firms in large cities and at airports, and they offer a variety of automobiles to suit your demands. To assure availability, it is essential to reserve your automobile in advance, especially during busy travel times.

- Cycling and Walking: Wiltshire is a great place for lovers of cycling and walking because of its beautiful scenery and vast network of routes. The county has a wide variety of cycling paths, from easy rides through the countryside to difficult off-road tracks. You can explore Wiltshire's natural beauty on foot thanks to the many footpaths and walking trails that are available.

Accommodation Options

There are many different types of lodging available in Wiltshire to accommodate various tastes and price ranges.

- Hotels: Wiltshire is home to a wide range of hotels that can meet diverse demands, from opulent resort hotels to inviting bed & breakfast inns. You can find lodging in old buildings, quiet country estates, or convenient city sites, all of which offer convenience and conveniences for a comfortable stay.

- Guesthouses and Bed and Breakfasts: These lodging options provide a more individualized and intimate experience in Wiltshire. These little lodgings are frequently family-run, offering gracious welcome and an opportunity to interact with the neighborhood. They are perfect for people looking for a warm and welcoming environment.

- Self-Catering Cottages: Self-catering cottages and vacation homes are available all around Wiltshire if you prefer more freedom and seclusion. You can cook your meals in these lodgings' fully furnished kitchens and have a home-away-from-home experience.

- Camping and Glamping: Wiltshire has a variety of campsites where you may pitch a tent or leave your caravan for those who enjoy the outdoors and being in the natural world. Some campgrounds also include glamping options, which let you take in the natural beauty while also having extra comforts and conveniences.

Travel Insurance

Consider travel insurance while making your Wiltshire travel arrangements. Travel insurance offers protection against unforeseeable occurrences like travel cancellations, medical emergencies, lost luggage, and other unanticipated circumstances. It is advised that you buy travel insurance that meets your requirements and offers sufficient coverage for your trip to Wiltshire. Review the policy's terms, limits of coverage, and exclusions thoroughly before buying insurance to be sure it meets your needs.

Having travel insurance gives you peace of mind and guarantees that you are covered in the event of any unanticipated events while you are in Wiltshire.

The optimum time to visit Wiltshire based on your tastes should be considered, as should your knowledge of visa requirements and your choice of the most practical form of transportation. You can embark on an unforgettable journey to see the enchanted landscapes, historical artifacts, and cultural wonders that Wiltshire has to offer with careful planning. Public transit, vehicle rentals, bicycle paths, and walking opportunities are just a few of the different ways to move around Wiltshire. The county offers a variety of lodging choices, including hotels, guesthouses, self-catering cottages, and camping grounds. To protect yourself and your things while visiting Wiltshire, it is advisable to think about getting travel insurance. You may totally immerse yourself in the beauties of this enchanting country once the logistics are taken care of.

CHAPTER THREE:
Exploring Wiltshire's Main Attractions

Wiltshire is home to a number of outstanding sites that highlight its rich history and magnificent architecture. When visiting Wiltshire, make sure not to miss these three major attractions:

Stonehenge

Unquestionably one of the most famous and enigmatic sites on earth is Stonehenge. The prehistoric stone circle has long captivated tourists. Approximately 5,000 years old and situated on Salisbury Plain, Stonehenge is a UNESCO World Heritage Site. Stonehenge's purpose and construction techniques continue to pique the interest of historians and researchers.

You can't help but be in awe of their magnificence and the sheer amount of labor that went into building them as you stand in front of the towering stone monoliths. The inner circle of stones is a magnificent sight, especially at sunrise or sunset when the stones produce striking shadows. The stones are arranged in a circular arrangement.

Stonehenge is a site of spiritual significance in addition to being a monument of early engineering. The visitor center's exhibits on the monument's history, theories, and builders are available for visitors to explore. It is really humbling to round the stone circle and think about its mysteries.

A famous landmark in Wiltshire and a masterpiece of medieval architecture is Salisbury Cathedral. This majestic cathedral, which is located in Salisbury, has been around for more than 800 years. It is well renowned for its towering spire, which is the highest in England at an astounding height of 123 meters (404 feet).

The cathedral's interior is filled with beautiful stained glass windows, finely carved stonework, and a contemplative ambiance. The Magna Carta, a significant historical document, is one of the original copies kept in the Chapter House.

You can get breath-taking panoramic views of Salisbury and the surrounding area by ascending the tower's spiral staircase. There are guided tours that offer information on the cathedral's history, architecture, and the people who were involved in its creation.

Avebury Stone Circle

The Avebury Stone Circle is a unique prehistoric site in Wiltshire that is close to the village of Avebury. The largest stone circle in all of Europe, it is a part of a bigger complex that includes the settlement and the surrounding area.

You can't help but be filled with awe as you stroll among the enormous standing stones and consider the prehistoric civilizations who built them. The Avebury Stone Circle is well-known for its enormous size, with the stones set in a circular arrangement and including a portion of the village within the circle. You can understand the complicated link between the stones, the landscape, and the people who built this sacred site by exploring the Avebury complex.

Wiltshire also has a plethora of additional historical and natural treasures in addition to these primary draws. Many charming market towns, including Marlborough and Bradford-on-Avon, can be found throughout the county, each of which has a special charm and historical value. It is enticing to explore the peaceful countryside with its undulating hills, meandering rivers, and quaint villages.

Longleat Safari Park, which is close to Warminster, is a great place for both families and wildlife aficionados to visit. With more than 9,000 acres of stunning parkland, it is one of the first safari parks established outside of Africa. You may go on an exhilarating safari trip here and get up close to a staggering variety of creatures from all over the world.

You'll see majestic lions, gorgeous giraffes, playful monkeys, and many other amazing animals as you travel around the safari park. The majestic Longleat House, a stately home with gorgeous grounds and a wealth of history to learn, is one of the park's numerous attractions. In a realistic and immersive setting, Longleat

Safari Park gives a unique opportunity to watch wildlife.

Lacock Abbey

Lacock Abbey is a unique historical landmark with an intriguing background and is situated in the quaint village of Lacock. The 13th-century abbey, which later became a family house, has fulfilled a variety of functions throughout its history. It is also known for its magnificently maintained medieval cloisters, which have appeared in a number of movies and television shows.

You can travel back in time by visiting Lacock Abbey and taking in its magnificent architecture. Explore the serene cloisters, stroll through the lovely gardens, and learn the fascinating lore surrounding this historic abbey. With its quaint alleyways, historic houses, and small stores, Lacock village is a treat to explore.

Salisbury Plain

Salisbury Plain is a compelling region that offers a rare fusion of natural beauty and historical value over a huge span of almost 300 square miles. This vast chalk plateau is well known for its extensive archaeological history, which includes a great number of old burial mounds, hill forts, and earthworks.

The plain also has a number of military training facilities, which heightens the sense of mystery and historical significance. You might occasionally see military drills and maneuvers going on, giving you a sense of the area's military history.

You may admire the Wiltshire countryside's pristine splendor by exploring Salisbury Plain. There is a sense of calm and tranquility brought about by the wide-open spaces, undulating hills, and panoramic views. It is the perfect location for hiking, biking, or just soaking in the gorgeous view while having a picnic.

The primary tourist destinations in Wiltshire, such as Stonehenge, Salisbury Cathedral, Avebury Stone Circle, Longleat Safari Park, Lacock Abbey, and Salisbury Plain, all bear witness to the county's rich historical and cultural past. By visiting these locations, you can get a peek of the distant past, learn about our predecessors' amazing accomplishments, and get up close and personal with some of the local fauna. Wiltshire is a place that will wow you at every step because there is so much more to learn about there.

CHAPTER FOUR:
Off the Beaten Path: Hidden Gems of Wiltshire

While Wiltshire is well known for its recognizable sites, there are still undiscovered treasures just waiting to be found. Explore these lesser-known sites that have their own special appeal and intrigue by going off the main path:

Stourhead Gardens

Stourhead Gardens is a gorgeous landscape garden that evokes the feeling of a secret paradise. It is tucked away amid the rolling hills of western Wiltshire. The gardens, created in the 18th century, are a beautiful fusion of the outdoors and classical architecture. You will come across tranquil lakes, flowing waterfalls, and enchanted grottoes as you explore the perfectly planted grounds.

The outstanding collection of rare and old specimens of exotic trees and plants at Stourhead Gardens has earned it worldwide renown. The Palladian palace, the focal point of the grounds, offers a look into the opulence of the past. Stourhead grounds promise a tranquil and picturesque refuge whether you explore the grounds in full bloom in the spring or take in the brilliant colors of autumn.

White Horse Hill

The famous Uffington White Horse resides on White Horse Hill, a knoll perched on the chalk downs close to Uffington. With its unusual shape carved into the hillside, this prehistoric hill figure, which dates back more than 3,000 years, is an amazing sight. The horse, which is easily recognizable from a great distance and has come to represent Wiltshire forever.

Beyond the White Horse, the surroundings' stunning views and an air of eerie antiquity are there. Visit the neighboring Uffington Castle, an Iron Age hillfort where you can stroll along the old ramparts and take in the expansive views. In addition to being a hidden jewel of Wiltshire, White Horse Hill is also an archaeological treasure rich in myth and history.

Silbury Hill

Near Avebury is the mysterious ancient mound known as Silbury Hill. It has been around for more than 4,500 years and is the largest prehistoric man-made mound in all of Europe. Silbury Hill, which rises to a height of 39 meters (130 feet), continues to be a fascinating archaeological puzzle because of the lack of knowledge on its initial use and construction methods.

Even if Silbury Hill isn't climbable, you can still behold its commanding presence and wonder what secrets it may be hiding. You may explore the area and take in the magnificence of this historic site thanks to the picturesque walking pathways that are available in the nearby countryside.

Westbury White Horse

Another amazing hill figure that merits attention is the Westbury White Horse, which is located on Wiltshire's western border. The horse, which is 55 meters (180 feet) long and carved into the chalk slope, is the largest and oldest white horse in Wiltshire. It is thought to have existed in the 1600s and is now a recognizable icon of the area.

You may take in expansive views of the surrounding countryside by going to the Westbury White Horse. You can trek to the top of the hill to view the expansive vistas and appreciate the natural beauty of Wiltshire.

Great Chalfield Manor

Great Chalfield Manor, a tranquil estate close to Melksham, is a well-kept secret that takes you back in time. With its enormous Great Hall, lovely gardens, and charming moat, this

15th-century manor home is a wonderful example of medieval architecture.

The Poyntz family, who have owned the land for more than 700 years, had a significant role in the history of the manor. You'll come across elaborate woodwork, priceless tapestries, and original details that offer a window into the past as you make your way through the house. The neighboring gardens provide a peaceful and scenic setting for a leisurely stroll with their vibrant flowers, well-kept lawns, and calming water features.

Bradford-on-Avon

Bradford-on-Avon, a historic town perched on the banks of the River Avon, is an undiscovered gem. It has an obvious old-world charm with its cobblestone streets, adorable cottages, and historic stone buildings. The majestic 14th-century Tithe Barn and the Saxon Church of St. Laurence are just two examples of the town's well-preserved architecture that will captivate you as you stroll around.

Admire the narrowboats floating over the water as you take a leisurely stroll down Bradford-on-Avon's scenic Kennet and Avon Canal. The town's charming boutiques, interesting cafes, and warm pubs offer an opportunity to unwind and take in the distinctive ambiance. Bradford-on-Avon is a hidden gem that perfectly encapsulates the allure of Wiltshire with its rich tradition and natural beauty.

The Kennet and Avon Canal is a serene waterway that connects the Rivers Thames and Avon, winding through the county of Wiltshire. The 87-mile-long canal provides a tranquil and beautiful getaway from the bustle of daily life. You can enjoy the surroundings at your own speed while cycling or taking leisurely walks along its quiet towpaths.

You'll find picturesque locks, quaint canalside communities, and tranquil waterways all along the canal. Herons, kingfishers, and ducks are commonly sighted along the canal's banks, making it a haven for wildlife. You can also rent a narrowboat or enjoy a leisurely boat ride to discover the delight of navigating the waterway firsthand.

The Kennet and Avon Canal offers a serene and beautiful route for discovering Wiltshire's secret nooks and taking in its natural splendor.

These undiscovered attractions, such as Stourhead Gardens, White Horse Hill, Silbury Hill, Westbury White Horse, Great Chalfield Manor, Bradford-on-Avon, and the Kennet and Avon Canal, provide a new viewpoint on Wiltshire's treasures. You can learn more about the county's rich history, natural beauty, and ancient mysteries by exploring these lesser-known destinations. You'll learn that Wiltshire has more to offer than you might initially think as you unearth these hidden gems.

CHAPTER FIVE:
Outdoor Adventures in Wiltshire

Wiltshire is the perfect place for outdoor enthusiasts looking for exhilarating activities and a connection with nature because of its diversified scenery and natural beauty. Wiltshire provides a wide range of possibilities to explore the great outdoors, whether you prefer walking, cycling, aquatic activities, or wildlife encounters:

Walking and Hiking Trails

There is a vast network of walking and hiking routes in Wiltshire that are suitable for people of all skill levels. Paths travel through gorgeous landscapes, old woodlands, and rolling hills as they cross the county. While the Wansdyke Path meanders through an old earthwork and provides panoramic views along the route, the Wiltshire White Horses Trail allows you to explore the famous white horses carved into the chalk downs.

The Salisbury Plain, with its intriguing archaeological sites and spacious landscapes, offers large stretches to explore. Another great place for walkers, with picturesque pathways and serene vistas, is the Cranborne Chase Area of Outstanding Natural Beauty. Wiltshire offers many possibilities to immerse yourself in its natural splendor, with paths that range from easy strolls to strenuous hikes.

There are several attractive cycling routes and designated trails in Wiltshire, making it a great place for cyclists to enjoy themselves. Cycling along the Kennet and Avon Canal Towpath provides stunning views of the canal and its environs while being relaxing. With its rocky terrain and rolling slopes, the North Wessex Downs Area of Outstanding Natural Beauty offers difficult off-road courses for mountain cyclists.

Wiltshire's picturesque villages and country lanes make for a lovely cycling experience for a more leisurely trip. You can journey into the Cotswolds, which extend into the county's northwest corner, or you can explore the Pewsey Vale and bike down the lovely River Wylye.

Wiltshire is a sanctuary for cyclists of all skill levels because of its diverse landscapes and well-maintained bicycle lanes.

The rivers, lakes, and canals of Wiltshire offer great chances for aquatic adventures. The Rivers Avon and Thames provide calm environments for canoeing, kayaking, and paddleboarding. You can get a unique perspective of Wiltshire's natural treasures as you paddle around the serene canals while admiring the beauty of the surroundings.

With its serene waterways, the Kennet and Avon Canal offers a serene environment for boating and canal cruising. Take a leisurely trip along the canal in a narrowboat, passing past quaint towns and picturesque locks. The county's rivers and lakes offer lots of possibilities for anglers to cast their lines and try their luck.

Wildlife and Nature Reserves

With a number of nature reserves and protected areas teeming with a variety of flora and fauna, Wiltshire is a paradise for wildlife aficionados. Excellent birdwatching chances are available at the RSPB reserves of Langford Lakes and Conigre Mead, where you may see a variety of species in their native surroundings.

Explore the Salisbury Plain to see uncommon bird species, deer, and wild ponies in their natural habitat. The Avon Valley Nature Reserve, which has boardwalk pathways and bird shelters for viewing, is a tranquil haven for wetland animals.

With their towering trees and diverse plant and animal life, the historic forests of Savernake Forest and West Woods offer a peaceful haven. The natural areas of Wiltshire provide a chance to get back in touch with nature and enjoy the wildlife's splendor.

In conclusion, Wiltshire has a wide range of outdoor activities for both nature lovers and excitement seekers. Wiltshire's varied landscapes offer countless possibilities to enjoy the great outdoors and make lifelong memories, from breathtaking walking and hiking trails to exhilarating cycling routes, peaceful water sports to wildlife encounters in nature reserves.

CHAPTER SIX:
Wiltshire's Historical and Cultural Sites

Wiltshire is rich in history and culture, and the county is home to numerous ancient buildings and opulent estates that provide a window into the past. Discover these outstanding places to get a sense of Wiltshire's fascinating history and cultural treasures:

Old Sarum

Old Sarum, a historic hill fort and the location of the first Salisbury Cathedral, is located on the outskirts of Salisbury. This ancient site, which dates back more than 5,000 years, offers a fascinating voyage through time. Discover the ruins of the Iron Age walls and stroll over the stunning ramparts, which provide sweeping views of the surrounding landscape.

Explore the ruins of the castle from the Middle Ages that once proudly stood atop the hill. Consider the religious events that were held inside the cathedral's walls prior to the construction of the modern Salisbury Cathedral as you delve into its past. Old Sarum offers a special chance to travel back in time and is a tribute to Wiltshire's rich history.

Wilton House

Wilton House, an opulent stately estate with a more than 400-year history, lies close to Salisbury. The great art collection, gorgeous interiors, and magnificent gardens of this Inigo Jones architectural masterpiece are well known.

You will experience the splendor of a bygone period as you tour the lavish rooms.

Admire the exquisite state chambers, such as the Double Cube Room, which are decorated with stunning paintings by illustrious painters. Admire the Palladian design and the elaborate wood carvings on the ceilings. Enter the beautifully groomed gardens outside to find sweeping lawns, decorative temples, and a peaceful water garden. The history, the art, and the beauty of nature are all abundant at Wilton House.

Bowood House and Gardens

Bowood House and Gardens, located in a sizable estate close to Calne, offer a delightful fusion of natural beauty, history, and culture. The Marquis and Marchioness of Lansdowne's ancestral residence, the Georgian house, is a remarkable example of Georgian architecture and interior design. Take in the antique furnishings, art collection, and famed Bowood library, which has a sizable collection of books and manuscripts.

Step outside into the Capability Brown-designed landscaped gardens and take in the breathtaking views, tranquil lakes, and bright floral displays. The Rhododendron Walk, Tractor Ted's Little Farm, and the Adventure Playground all offer family-friendly entertainment. Bowood House and Gardens offers a fun day trip where history, culture, and natural beauty all come together.

Malmesbury monastery, a magnificent medieval monastery that bears witness to centuries of ecclesiastical and architectural history, is situated in the lovely market town of Malmesbury. The abbey, which dates back more than a thousand years, has beautiful Gothic architecture and a long history. The grand nave, beautiful stained glass windows, and elaborate ceiling vaults will astound you as you enter.

Discover hidden chapels and graves that provide insight into the abbey's past as you explore the nooks and crannies of the building. Visit the Abbey House Gardens, which have lovely blossoms and serene areas, or climb the tower for sweeping views of the surrounding landscape. Malmesbury Abbey is a location with significant historical and spiritual value that provides a window into Wiltshire's past.

Devizes Castle

Devizes Castle is a historic medieval fortification that is located in the Devizes town. The fortress, which Roger of Salisbury built in the 12th century, was strategically important in the town's defense. The castle's imposing earthwork fortifications and remaining portions of the keep nevertheless survive as a reminder of its previous splendor even though much of the castle's original structure is now in ruins.

Take a stroll around the castle grounds and try to picture the sieges and wars that took place within. Enjoy sweeping views of the town and the surroundings from the top of the earthworks.

Devizes Castle provides a window into Wiltshire's military past and the engineering prowess of medieval defenses.

Trowbridge Museum

The Trowbridge Museum, which is situated in the town of Trowbridge, exhibits the industrial and social history of the community and the surrounding area. The museum, located in a former mill, features hands-on exhibits, antiques, and installations that trace the development of Trowbridge throughout the Industrial Revolution from a sleepy village to a flourishing hub of textile manufacture.

Learn about the life of the workers and the effects of the textile industry on the community as you explore the replica of a mill worker's house. Through exhibitions that illustrate the industrial accomplishments, social history, and cultural traditions of Trowbridge, learn more about its rich heritage. The Trowbridge Museum offers enlightening details about the town's past and its importance in Wiltshire's history.

You can learn more about the rich history and architectural riches of Wiltshire by visiting these historical and cultural places, such as Old Sarum, Wilton House, Bowood House and Gardens, Malmesbury Abbey, Devizes Castle, and the Trowbridge Museum. Wiltshire's historical and cultural attractions, which range from imposing stately estates to old hill forts, serve as reminders of the county's rich history and continuing legacy.

CHAPTER SEVEN: Exploring Wiltshire's Towns and Villages

The county of Wiltshire is home to a number of quaint cities and lovely villages that highlight the area's own personality and provide a fascinating fusion of history, culture, and natural beauty. Discover the towns and villages listed below to fully experience Wiltshire:

Salisbury

The city of Salisbury, which is located in the county of Wiltshire, is a thriving cultural center and a starting point for visits to some of the region's most well-known landmarks. Visit the lively market square, stroll through the ancient alleyways lined with timber-framed buildings, and marvel at the majestic Salisbury Cathedral, a masterpiece of medieval construction that holds the renowned Magna Carta.

Explore the picturesque Mompesson House and The Salisbury Museum, both of which provide insights into the city's background, as you stroll through the lovely Salisbury Cathedral Close. Discover the tranquil Salisbury Water Meadows, then stroll along the Avon River. Salisbury is a must-see location in Wiltshire because of its blend of historical sites, cultural assets, and natural beauty.

Marlborough

Marlborough is a charming market town with a rich history and a lively atmosphere that is located on the edge of the North Wessex Downs

Area of Outstanding Natural Beauty. Visit the 15th-century St. Peter's Church, which offers panoramic views from its tower, and stroll down the broad High Street, which is studded with Georgian houses and quaint stores.

Explore the grounds of the esteemed independent Marlborough College and the Marlborough Museum to learn more about the town's unique past. A leisurely stroll along the Kennet and Avon Canal is recommended. You may also visit the neighboring Savernake Forest, which is renowned for its old trees and peaceful walking paths. Marlborough is an intriguing location due to its blend of history, natural beauty, and dynamic charm.

The market town of Devizes, which is located in rural Wiltshire, is bursting with personality and historical interest. Investigate the crowded market square where you may buy regional foods, handmade items, and antiques. Take a tour of the Wadworth Brewery, a family-run business that has been brewing traditional ales since 1875, to learn about the brewing process and to try some of their renowned brews.

Visit the Wiltshire Museum, which features objects from the county's prehistoric past to the present, to fully immerse yourself in the town's history. Keep in mind to visit the famous Devizes Locks, a flight of 29 locks on the Kennet and Avon Canal that offers a fascinating look at the engineering marvels of the canal system.

The majestic Devizes Castle, whose ruins provide a peek into the town's medieval past, is also located in Devizes. Devizes is a hidden gem just waiting to be discovered with its charming history, lively market, and unique sights.

Bradford-on-Avon

Bradford-on-Avon is a lovely town that oozes old-world charm. It is located along the banks of the River Avon. The village is a treat to visit because of its charming cottages, quiet waterway, and ancient architecture. Explore the small lanes dotted with honey-colored stone structures, cross the bridge from the fourteenth century, and stop to gaze at the Saxon Church and Tithe Barn.

Visit the Bradford-on-Avon Museum to fully immerse yourself in the history of the community. The museum features interesting exhibits that explain the town's history. Take a lovely canal boat ride or go for a stroll along the river to take in the tranquil atmosphere. Bradford-on-Avon is a town that will take you back in time with its timeless beauty and rich history.

Lacock

Visit the charming village of Lacock, renowned for its beautifully preserved medieval architecture, and travel back in time. The everlasting appeal of this traditional English village has led to its use as the setting for a number of film and television projects. You'll have the impression that you've entered a live postcard as you stroll around the streets.

Discover Lacock Abbey, a former nunnery turned stately mansion with gorgeous cloisters, lovely gardens, and an interesting past. With its tiny stores, quaint taverns, and attractive houses, the hamlet itself is a treat to explore. Lacock is a must-visit location for history aficionados and photography enthusiasts due to its natural beauty and historical significance.

Castle Combe

One of England's prettiest villages, Castle Combe is located in the Cotswolds Area of Outstanding Natural Beauty. It's simple to understand why with its honey-colored stone homes, flower-filled gardens, and picture-perfect rural location. The village's ageless beauty and quiet atmosphere will enthrall you as you stroll around it.

Admire the 14th-century St. Andrew's Church's splendor, wander by the bubbling Bybrook River, and marvel at the ancient Market Cross. It's easy to see why Castle Combe has won over the hearts of both tourists and filmmakers thanks to its pristine atmosphere, which has made it a favorite movie site.

You can sample the various cuisines of Wiltshire by traveling to these cities and villages, such as Salisbury, Marlborough, Devizes, Bradford-on-Avon, Lacock, and Castle Combe. The cities and villages of Wiltshire provide a lovely blend of history, culture, and natural beauty, making them essential components of any trip to the county. These include the famous landmarks of Salisbury, the lively streets of market towns, and the tranquil charm of rural villages.

CHAPTER EIGHT:
Wiltshire's Culinary Delights

Wiltshire enchants with its natural beauty, historical sites, and gastronomic offers in addition to tantalizing the taste buds. The county offers a fantastic culinary experience, from locally grown products to quaint pubs and lively food festivals. Here are some of the gastronomic highlights of Wiltshire:

Local Food and Produce

Wiltshire has a long history of farming, and its fertile ground yields an abundance of healthy foods. High-quality meats from the county, like luscious lamb, flavorful beef, and the well-known Wiltshire cured ham, are well-known. Discover the best of Wiltshire's products by visiting nearby farms and farm stores, where you can try artisan cheeses, locally produced vegetables, and award-winning ciders and beers.

Traditional Pubs and Restaurants

There are several little bars and eateries in Wiltshire that highlight the area's culinary traditions. Experience the welcoming atmosphere and delicious pub meals, including traditional Sunday roasts, pies, and fish & chips. To make recipes that honor the flavors of Wiltshire, several eateries use locally sourced products.

Visit one of Wiltshire's well-known restaurants for a fine dining experience where skilled chefs combine traditional and modern cooking methods to produce delectable delicacies. These restaurants showcase the county's culinary skills with inventive tasting menus and seasonal treats.

Farmers' Markets

Farmers' markets in Wiltshire offer a chance to find a variety of regional foods, handcrafted goods, and homemade delicacies. These markets are a hive of activity and provide a lively environment where you can meet local farmers, try their products, and buy fresh, seasonal items. Wiltshire's farmers markets are a foodie's paradise, offering everything from freshly baked bread to organic veggies, artisan cheeses, and homemade jams.

The county of Wiltshire often holds a variety of food festivals to honor its rich culinary history. These events offer a chance to sample the best flavors of the area while showcasing regional growers, chefs, and culinary artisans. These events offer a feast for the senses with everything from food and beverage tastings to cooking demos and live entertainment.

The Devizes Food and Drink Festival is one significant event that highlights the best of regional and local produce through a number of activities, such as pop-up markets, beer and cider festivals, and themed dining experiences. The Salisbury Food and Drink Festival, which offers a variety of gastronomic delights, from street food booths to chef demos, is another highlight.

The vibrant culinary scene in Wiltshire is a result of the area's long agricultural history, dedication to using local ingredients, and inventive cooking. You'll find a varied and delightful culinary scene that genuinely captures the flavors of Wiltshire, whether you're feasting in traditional pub grub, touring farmers' markets, or immersing yourself in vibrant food festivals.

CHAPTER NINE:
Shopping and Souvenirs in Wiltshire

You can take a little of Wiltshire's charm home by purchasing at one of the many unusual stores you'll come across while visiting the county. Wiltshire offers a wide variety of possibilities for selecting the ideal souvenir, from regional art and crafts to antiques, farm shops, and gift shops. Here are some of Wiltshire's shopping's highlights:

Local Art and Crafts

There is a plethora of regional art and crafts that exquisitely capture the county's landscapes and history in Wiltshire, a home for artists and craftspeople. Explore local artists' galleries and independent shops that feature paintings, sculptures, ceramics, and textiles. You can choose from a variety of items that perfectly represent the spirit of Wiltshire's inventiveness, whether you're looking for an eye-catching piece of art or a handcrafted item.

Antiques and Vintage Shops

Wiltshire is well-known for its extensive history, and vintage and antique shops provide a wealth of unusual items. Browse through a variety of antique furniture, vintage apparel, collectibles, and curiosities to uncover hidden gems and delve into history. These stores offer an intriguing window into Wiltshire's history, whether you're a serious collector or just looking for a sentimental souvenir.

Farm Shops and Delis

Wiltshire's farm stores and delis, where you can find a wealth of locally sourced and handmade goods, commemorate the county's agricultural heritage. These businesses provide a wide variety of fresh foods, such as locally sourced meats, cheeses, baked products, seasonal fruits and vegetables, and fruits and vegetables from the region. Pick up some delicious delicacies to enjoy during your visit or to take home as edible keepsakes to help local farmers and revel in Wiltshire's delights.

Gift Shops

The gift shops in Wiltshire are a veritable gold mine of one-of-a-kind and carefully chosen products. These shops provide a variety of possibilities for selecting the ideal souvenir of your trip to Wiltshire, from delightful trinkets to handcrafted crafts. Look through a selection of trinkets crafted by hand, including handmade jewelry, postcards, and keychains with local themes. A wide range of goods that highlight Wiltshire's cultural past are also available, including publications on the region's history, traditional crafts, and even locally produced cosmetics.

Wiltshire's shopping environment offers a wide range of choices, whether you're looking for fine art, antiques, gourmet treats, or unique presents. You may bring a little of Wiltshire's charm home and help the neighborhood at the same time by patronizing local artisans, farmers, and small businesses. To locate that unique souvenir that will remind you of your amazing stay in

Wiltshire, make sure to set aside some time to browse the local shops.

CHAPTER TEN:
Festivals and Events in
Wiltshire

Wiltshire is a lively county that offers numerous festivals and events all year long, drawing tourists from close and far. These festivals of the arts, culture, music, and entertainment provide a rich experience that highlights the county's inventiveness and sense of civic engagement. The following Wiltshire celebrations and events are noteworthy:

Salisbury International Arts Festival

The Salisbury International Arts Festival, which brings together artists, performers, and spectators for a diverse program of music, dance, theater, visual arts, and more, is a high point on the cultural calendar. This well-known festival presents inventive performances and exhibitions at various locations throughout Salisbury, showcasing a wide variety of local and international talent. The festival offers a diverse tapestry of creative experiences, from enthralling theater productions to breathtaking dance performances and provocative art installations.

Devizes International Street Festival

The Devizes International Street Festival turns the old town into a dynamic stage as it celebrates street art, music, and circus performances. Street performances, acrobatics, live music, and dance acts from all over the world are all available for spectators to enjoy. The festival also features parades, workshops, and kid-friendly interactive activities. Devizes' streets come alive with an artistic flair that welcomes both residents and visitors to take part in the festive ambiance.

Chippenham Folk Festival

An exciting festival that honors the vibrant history of folk music, dance, and traditional arts is the Chippenham Folk Festival. This four-day event offers a comprehensive schedule of concerts, workshops, ceilidhs (traditional dances), discussions, and street performers. To celebrate the variety of folk traditions and to share their talents, musicians, dancers, and aficionados meet together. The Chippenham Folk Festival provides a remarkable experience chock-full of upbeat music and contagious energy, whether you're an experienced fan of folk music or merely inquisitive about this dynamic genre.

The Wiltshire Music and Drama Festival is an annual occasion that offers local artists of all ages and skill levels a stage on which to display their abilities in music, drama, and spoken word. Participants have the option of competing in competitive categories or giving non-competitive performances while receiving insightful criticism from knowledgeable adjudicators. In addition to celebrating the performing arts, this festival fosters artistic development and a sense of community among artists and audiences.

These Wiltshire festivals and events serve as a reminder of the county's dedication to promoting artistic expression, cultural diversity, and neighborhood involvement. They provide chances for residents and guests to interact, enjoy acts of the highest caliber, and recognize the creative skills of the area. The festivals and events in Wiltshire will enthrall and inspire you whether you love the arts, enjoy music, or are just looking for a really immersive cultural experience.

CHAPTER ELEVEN:
Practical Information for
Travelers

A seamless and pleasurable journey to Wiltshire depends on having useful information at your fingertips when making travel plans. Here are some important factors to think about:

Accommodation Options

There are many different types of lodging available in Wiltshire to accommodate a variety of tastes and price ranges. There is accommodation for everyone, including five-star hotels, lovely bed and breakfasts, self-catering cottages, and campgrounds. There are numerous hotels, guesthouses, and boutique lodging options in well-known tourist destinations including Salisbury and Bath. Consider staying in one of the county's charming villages or rural getaways if you'd want a more rural experience. It's advisable to make reservations in advance to ensure your preferred lodging, especially during busy travel times.

Transportation in Wiltshire

Wiltshire has an efficient transportation system, making getting throughout the county very simple. The closest major airports for air travel are Southampton Airport and Bristol Airport, both of which provide domestic and international flights. To get to your destination in Wiltshire from there, you can rent a car, board a train, or take a bus.

Buses and railways are available for public transit within the county, with frequent routes linking towns and villages. It is simple to explore the area thanks to the Wiltshire Council's comprehensive bus network. Salisbury, Chippenham, Trowbridge, and Swindon have train stations that connect to the county's major towns and cities.

Money and Currency Exchange

The British Pound (GBP) is the official unit of currency in the United Kingdom. In many towns and cities across Wiltshire, there are ATMs where you may use your debit or credit card to withdraw cash. Hotels, restaurants, and retail establishments all accept major credit and debit cards. To prevent any problems with card transactions, it's always a good idea to let your bank or credit card company know about your vacation plans.

Banks and specialized currency exchange offices offer currency exchange services, especially in larger towns and cities. To make sure you get the best value for your money, it is advisable to compare exchange rates and fees.

Language and Cultural Etiquette

The majority of people in Wiltshire and the rest of the UK speak English. You won't have any trouble interacting with residents or using services as a visitor. Though it never hurts to learn a few basic words and phrases in the local tongue, as with any travel destination, doing so can improve your interactions with locals.

When entering stores, restaurants, or striking up a discussion, it's courteous to say "hello" or "good morning/afternoon/evening" to the person you're speaking to. The standard gratuity in restaurants is between 10% and 15% of the total cost for excellent service. It's also considerate to wait patiently in line and respect others' personal space.

It's crucial to dress modestly and properly while entering someone's home or visiting a place of worship. Asking for permission before taking pictures is also polite, especially in private or revered areas.

You can guarantee a pleasant and polite experience while visiting Wiltshire by paying attention to regional customs and cultural etiquette.

These helpful travel suggestions can assist you in navigating Wiltshire and maximizing your trip. You'll be well-prepared to take advantage of the beauty, history, and hospitality that Wiltshire has to offer by thinking about lodging alternatives, knowing transportation, handling cash, and being mindful of cultural norms.

CHAPTER TWELVE:
Safety and Health in Wiltshire

When traveling anywhere, it's crucial to ensure your safety and wellbeing, and Wiltshire is no different. To provide guests with a relaxing and safe stay, the county upholds a high standard of safety and provides dependable health services. Here are some crucial considerations for Wiltshire's health and safety:

Emergency Contacts

Knowing the appropriate contact numbers is crucial in the event of an emergency. Dial 999 to contact the emergency services in the United Kingdom. Depending on the emergency, calling this number will link you to the police, fire department, or ambulance services. You can call the non-emergency police line at (101), if you need assistance but the issue is not an imminent emergency.

Although Wiltshire is generally thought of as a safe place for tourists to visit, it is always advisable to exercise common sense caution. Following are some general safety recommendations:

- Pay attention to your surroundings, particularly when it's busy or late at night in tourist areas.

- Protect your personal items, and be on the lookout for pickpockets.

- Make use of trustworthy taxi services and legal vehicles.

- At popular tourist destinations like national parks and Stonehenge, heed any safety advice or cautions.

- If you intend to hike or explore a remote area, tell someone about your plans and bring the necessary supplies, clothing, and maps.

You can contribute to making sure that your trip to Wiltshire is safe and enjoyable by being cautious and using common sense.

Both residents and visitors in Wiltshire have access to a dependable healthcare system with a variety of medical services and facilities. You can get medical advice and treatment at a walk-in clinic or from your neighborhood general practitioner (GP) if you have non-emergency medical issues. It's a good idea to obtain travel insurance that will pay for any potential medical costs you may incur while traveling.

In most towns and cities in Wiltshire, you'll find pharmacies (sometimes called chemists). In addition to providing prescription and over-the-counter medicines, pharmacies also provide advice on minor illnesses. During your appointment, they can also offer advice on any particular health issues you may have.

It's generally advisable to get complete travel insurance that addresses both potential cancellations and unanticipated circumstances, as well as medical emergencies. Make sure you have all the immunizations your doctor has advised and that you have your prescription drugs with you before your travel.

You can get rapid help in case of a medical emergency by dialing 999 for emergency services.

You can feel secure throughout your visit to Wiltshire by being aware of emergency contacts, following safety precautions, and having access to medical services. Prioritizing your safety and wellbeing will enable you to fully take advantage of the county's attractions and experiences.

CHAPTER THIRTEEN:
Conclusion and Farewell to Wiltshire

We hope that as you have read through the pages of this travel book, it has given you a thorough insight of the charming county of Wiltshire. Wiltshire provides a wealth of activities that will make a lasting impact, from its alluring landscapes and historical treasures to its hidden gems and active culture.

We have covered Wiltshire's geography, climate, and weather in-depth throughout this book so that you can enjoy the county's varied natural beauties. We have looked at the rich history, diverse cultural heritage, and variety of festivals and activities that unite the neighborhood in joy.

You've learned about the top sights that draw tourists from all over the world, like the famous Stonehenge, the magnificent Salisbury Cathedral, and the historic Avebury Stone Circle. We've also strayed off the road, discovering undiscovered treasures like the serene Stourhead Gardens, the fascinating White Horse Hill, and the mysterious Silbury Hill.

The county's walking and hiking trails, cycling routes, aquatic sports, and abundance of animals and nature reserves will appeal to outdoor explorers. History buffs will like the amazing historical and cultural monuments, which include the Old Sarum ruins, Wilton House's opulence, and the mesmerizing beauty of Bowood House and Gardens.

Salisbury, Marlborough, Devizes, Bradford-on-Avon, Lacock, and Castle Combe are just a few of the magnificent towns and villages we have visited; each has its own special charm and personality.

Wiltshire's native foods and products, quaint pubs and eateries, farmers' markets, and food festivals showcasing the county's culinary treasures have enticed your taste buds.

You've learned about possibilities to immerse yourself in regional arts and crafts, hunt for vintage treasures in antique stores, and locate the ideal gifts in Wiltshire's farm shops, delis, and gift shops.

The Salisbury International Arts Festival, Devizes International Street Festival,

Chippenham Folk Festival, and Wiltshire Music and Drama Festival are just a few of the exciting festivals and events we've highlighted to help you fully experience the county's vibrant culture.

You may navigate Wiltshire with ease thanks to the useful information that has been provided, such as lodging possibilities, travel information, currency conversion information, and cultural etiquette.

We've talked about how important health and safety are, making sure you are ready with emergency contact information, safety advice, and awareness of the medical facilities and pharmacies in Wiltshire.

We wish you well as you say goodbye to Wiltshire and that the memories and encounters you had there will live on in your heart forever. May the splendor and allure of this wonderful county linger in your heart and entice you to return in the future to discover even more of its beauties.

Safe travels, and may your upcoming journey be blessed with happiness, learning, and an exploratory spirit!

Farewell, dear traveler, and may Wiltshire's magic always be etched in your memories.

CHAPTER FOURTEEN:
Appendix

In this appendix section, you will find additional resources and tools to enhance your experience while exploring Wiltshire. These include useful phrases in English, websites for further information, a currency conversion chart, and a packing list to ensure you have everything you need for your trip.

30 Useful Phrases in English and Pronunciations

- Hello. [həˈləʊ]

- Thank you. [θæŋk juː]

- Excuse me. [ɪkˈskjuːz miː]

- Please. [pliːz]

- Yes. [jes]

- No. [nəʊ]

- I'm sorry. [aɪm ˈsɒri]

- Could you help me, please? [kʊd juː hɛlp miː pliːz]

- Where is...? [weər ɪz]

- How much does it cost? [haʊ mʌt ˈdʌz ɪt kɒst]

- I would like... [aɪ wʊd laɪk]

- Can you recommend a good restaurant? [kæn juː ˌrɛkəˈmɛnd ə gʊd ˈrɛstrɒnt]

- What time does it open/close? [wɒt taɪm ˈdʌz ɪt ˈəʊpən/kləʊz]

- Where can I find a pharmacy? [weər kæn aɪ faɪnd ə ˈfɑːməsiː]

- I need a doctor. [aɪ niːd ə ˈdɒktə]

- Could you speak more slowly, please? [kʊd juː spiːk mɔː ˈsləʊli pliːz]

- What is your name? [wɒt ɪz jɔːr neɪm]

- Nice to meet you. [naɪs tuː miːt juː]

- Where is the nearest ATM? [weər ɪz ðiː ˈnɪərɪst eɪtiːˈɛm]

- Can you help me with directions? [kæn juː hɛlp miː wɪð dɪˈrɛkʃənz]

- What is the Wi-Fi password? [wɒt ɪz ðə ˈwaɪfaɪ ˈpɑːswɜːd]

- Is there a public restroom nearby? [ɪz ðeər ə ˈpʌblɪk ˈrɛstruːm ˈnɪəbaɪ]

- I don't understand. [aɪ dəʊnt ˌʌndəˈstænd]

- Where can I buy tickets? [weər kæn aɪ baɪ ˈtɪkɪts]

- Can you take a photo of me, please? [kæn juː teɪk ə ˈfəʊtəʊ əv miː pliːz]

- Cheers! [tʃɪəz]

- Goodbye. [ɡʊdˈbaɪ]

- Have a nice day. [hæv ə naɪs deɪ]

Note: The above pronunciations are provided in parentheses for guidance.

Useful Websites

VisitWiltshire:

www.visitwiltshire.co.uk

Wiltshire Council:

www.wiltshire.gov.uk

English Heritage:

www.english-heritage.org.uk

National Trust:

www.nationaltrust.org.uk

These websites provide valuable information on attractions, events, transportation, and accommodations in Wiltshire. They are excellent resources for planning your itinerary and staying up to date with the latest happenings in the county.

Currency Conversion Chart

Below is a conversion chart to help you convert common currencies into British pounds (GBP) for your reference:

- US Dollar (USD) = 0.72 GBP
- Euro (EUR) = 0.85 GBP
- Canadian Dollar (CAD) = 0.58 GBP
- Australian Dollar (AUD) = 0.52 GBP
- Japanese Yen (JPY) = 0.0065 GBP
- Swiss Franc (CHF) = 0.70 GBP

Please note that exchange rates may vary, so it's advisable to check the current rates before making any currency conversions.

Packing List

To ensure you have everything you need for your trip to Wiltshire, consider including the following items in your packing list:

- Clothing suitable for the season (including layers for varying weather conditions)
- Comfortable walking shoes
- Rainproof jacket or umbrella
- Sunscreen and hat for sun protection
- Travel adapter for electrical outlets
- Travel guidebook or map of Wiltshire
- Camera or smartphone for capturing memories
- Prescription medications, if applicable
- Travel insurance documents
- Any necessary travel documents (passport, visa, ID cards)
- Cash and/or credit cards

Feel free to personalize the packing list based on your specific needs and activities planned during your visit.

By utilizing these resources and being well-prepared, you can make the most of your time in Wiltshire, ensuring a smooth and enjoyable journey.

Printed in Great Britain
by Amazon

24665522R00066